Original title:

Tangled Tendrils

Copyright © 2025 Creative Arts Management OÜ
All rights reserved.

Author: Dexter Sullivan
ISBN HARDBACK: 978-1-80581-791-8
ISBN PAPERBACK: 978-1-80581-318-7
ISBN EBOOK: 978-1-80581-791-8

Overgrown Reveries

In the garden, where weeds play,
Hiding secrets in disarray.
Rabbits dance, unkempt their hair,
Chasing shadows, without a care.

Sunflowers sing at the moon's jest,
Twirling blooms, putting dreams to test.
Laughter hides in the green abyss,
Nature's giggle, an endless bliss.

Bound by the Undergrowth

Underneath vines, a fox does snooze,
Waking up to a world confused.
Beneath the leaves, a party brews,
With acorns tossed and laughter too.

Squirrels slip in their wonky boots,
While bumblebees play polka flute.
A picnic lost in leafy layers,
As nature's whimsy leads to players.

Labyrinth of Lushness

Wander through hedges, find a snack,
In this maze, we never look back.
Cucumbers gossip, tomatoes grin,
Rambunctious plants let the chaos begin.

A snail races with a giggling ant,
On this journey, who needs to chant?
Fuzzy hedgehogs trade silly tales,
While mischief hides in the leafy trails.

Gnarled Embrace

Twisted branches twist the mind,
Where a sense of humor's easy to find.
Laughter echoes through knotted roots,
As gnomes wear hats that bring down hoots.

In this tangle of quirky sights,
Frogs croak jokes under starry nights.
Every twist brings comedy's cheer,
The woods are alive with laughter here.

The Fabric of the Forest

In the woods, a squirrel ran,
Chasing shadows with a plan.
He met a fox who danced around,
Then tripped on roots that hit the ground.

A bird up high began to sing,
Of leafy hats and funny bling.
The branches waved, a silly show,
As nature's laughter starts to flow.

Embrace of the Wild

In the grass, a rabbit pranced,
While butterflies just twirled and danced.
The flowers giggled, colors bright,
As bees buzzed in a funny flight.

A bear rolled by, a clumsy sight,
Chasing dreams in broad daylight.
With honey pots that slipped and slid,
He laughed and danced, a happy kid.

Climbing Shadows

A cat on branches tried to climb,
But lost its grip, oh what a crime!
It tangled up in vines so green,
And mumbled things that were quite mean.

The sun looked down and winked with glee,
As shadows danced beneath the tree.
With every flap and flutter there,
The forest rang with jokers' flair.

Crescendo of Greenery

The trees held hands and spun around,
As acorns fell without a sound.
The grass tickled passing feet,
While frogs made leaps in rhythmic beat.

A party brewed 'neath leafy grooves,
Where critters danced their silly moves.
With nature's band, the fun won't cease,
In this green world, we find our peace.

Whispers in the Vines

In the garden, vines do chat,
They gossip daily, just like that.
Chasing bugs and sunlit rays,
In their silly, twisty ways.

Laughter echoes through the leaves,
As they plot their playful thieves.
With a flick they pull and sway,
Tripping toes at close of day.

Nature's Knotted Embrace

Ropes of green and sprigs of cheer,
Hugging trees and feeling near.
Branches tickle, vines take flight,
What a mess, but what a sight!

A squirrel dances on the line,
While flowers wink and call it fine.
Nature's embrace, all jumbled tight,
It's a circus, what a delight!

Threads of Sunlight

Sunbeams dip and weave through green,
In this dance, oh what a scene!
Twirling, spinning with delight,
Nature's game, so fun, so bright.

A spider grins, her web a mess,
Who can blame her? She's the best!
With threads of gold that glisten bold,
Each strand a story waiting to be told.

Interwoven Dreams

Dreams entwined on leafy beds,
Where laughter flows and joy spreads.
Chasing clouds, they trip and fall,
Nature's playroom, loved by all.

They reach for stars, then tumble down,
Giggles echo all around.
Each flopped attempt a tale to share,
In this dance of joyous flair.

The Winding Way

In a garden of giggles, roots do dance,
Wobbling weeds take a clumsy stance.
Rabbits smile as they trip on vines,
Nature's jesters in quirky designs.

Bumbling bugs in a twirling maze,
Making mischief in playful ways.
A snail slides by with a curious peek,
While flowers chuckle, their laughter unique.

Stories in the Veil

Behind the leaves, tales intertwine,
A caterpillar claims, 'This leaf is mine!'
The sunbeam winks at the shyest sprout,
Whispering secrets it can't live without.

A spider weaves with a pun or two,
"My webs are better, they're shiny and new!"
The breeze tickles, making petals sway,
Nature's jesters in a feathery play.

The Veined Narrative

Roots are scribbling beneath the ground,
Writing stories that twirl and abound.
A worm narrates with a giggly squirm,
As mushrooms chuckle in their quirky term.

Leaves turn pages in a fluttering race,
While squirrels compete for a nutty embrace.
Each vine has a voice in a comic tone,
Sharing tales that they claim as their own.

Growth's Labyrinth

In a maze of green where laughter's sprout,
Bouncing beetles scream, 'No way out!'
Chasing critters in a zigzag spree,
As daisies giggle, 'Come dance with me!'

The paths are silly, with glee they twist,
Throwing parties that none could resist.
A parade of petals, all dressed to play,
In the great green maze where hilarity stays.

Fragments of Flora

In the garden's chaotic spree,
Plants dance like they're full of glee.
If roses could laugh, oh what a sight,
Petals giggling, taking flight.

Cacti wearing hats so grand,
They poke at clouds with their prickly hand.
The daisies play tag and run round,
While violets whisper, giggles abound.

Sunflowers strut in the morning light,
Swinging their heads, oh what a sight!
In this patch of whimsy, colors collide,
Nature's own circus, nothing to hide.

So let's raise a toast to this plant parade,
Where even the weeds are not afraid.
For in this garden of laughter and cheer,
Every leaf whispers, "We're glad you're here!"

The Wild Embrace

Who knew vines could be such a tease?
Wrapping around legs with perfect ease.
They prance and they sway, oh what a show,
Entwined in a twirl, too wild to know.

Ferns holding hands in a leafy hug,
Telling tales while snug as a bug.
The flowers gossip and roll their eyes,
As bees buzz by with a wobbly rise.

Bamboo shoots crack jokes that go on and on,
While mushrooms dance until the dawn.
A cacophony of green and of fun,
In this wild embrace, we all feel young.

So join the party, don't be shy,
In this wild wonder, give it a try.
For nature's laughter, loud and free,
Binds us together in pure glee!

The Knot of Kin

In the garden, roots entwine,
Laughing branches, oh so fine.
Cousins clash with playful glee,
Poking fun at Auntie Bee.

Silly vines in a twisty race,
Bouncing blooms in a cheeky space.
Uncle Thistle claims the ground,
While cousins shout, "Where's the sound?"

Grandpa Moss tells silly tales,
Of woodland whispers and crazy snails.
All together, they won't split,
In this knot, they find their wit.

Stories in the Leaves

Rustling pages of green delight,
Whispered secrets take flight.
Squirrels chit-chat, life a jest,
Nature's comedy, truly blessed.

Each leaf tells a funny line,
Of pranks through summer, oh divine!
A tale of acorns on the run,
Gathering laughter, oh what fun!

Wind chuckles, a playful howl,
As branches sway, an old owl growls.
Under this canopy, joy spreads wide,
Every flutter filled with pride.

Embracing the Barbs

Thorns that giggle, quite absurd,
Mocking beauty without a word.
Poking fun and pointing out,
The irony that makes us shout.

Cacti wear their prickly hats,
While yonder daisies share their chats.
Pansy pickers skip away,
Avoiding barbs on sunny day.

Gathered at the thorny spree,
Barbed banter, oh so free!
Nature's jesters, who would know,
That prickles spread the joy and glow?

Journeys Between the Branches

Swaying high, the branches dance,
Inviting birds to take a chance.
Fluttering wings, a joyful sound,
Adventures high above the ground.

A monkey swings with silly flair,
Chasing leaves without a care.
Each leap is filled with guffaw,
Nature's playground has no flaw.

Scratching bark tells of the trips,
Of lonely squirrels and acorn flips.
Through the canopy, a laughter trail,
In this wild, we shall prevail.

Braided Reflections

In the garden, weeds chatter,
While flowers laugh, like a clatter.
A vine twists round its own face,
Says, "I'm winning this race!"

Leaves exchange gossip at night,
About a snail's sluggish flight.
Sunshine gives them all a cheer,
While the clouds just stand in jeer.

Petals in polka dots sway,
Dancing like it's a cabaret.
Yet roots below them sigh,
"We're stuck here, oh my, oh my!"

It's a circus of green delight,
With nature playing its own sight.
When growth gets a little silly,
You can't help but chuckle, really!

The Conflicted Canopy

Beneath branches, shadows fight,
Is it day or is it night?
Squirrels debate over nuts galore,
While branches swing like a door.

A branch complains about its height,
"I can't see that starry light!"
The leaves whisper back in glee,
"Don't worry, just let it be!"

The wind plays tag, then takes a nap,
While bugs crawl in a funny clap.
A woodpecker joins in the fun,
Foolishness under the sun!

With laughter ringing through the air,
Each tree has its own little flair.
Nature's comedy, in full bloom,
Makes you forget all gloom and doom!

Roots Underfoot

Down below where no one sees,
Roots gossip like busy bees.
"Did you hear about the tree?
Seems quite giddy, doesn't he?"

They tangle and wiggle with flair,
Sometimes they trip on their own hair.
One root says, "I can't go on,
I'm caught up in this jungle con!"

While worms wait for the ground's applause,
They're the real show without a pause.
"Pull up a seat, it's quite the show,
As we flaunt where no one can go!"

So every time you stomp around,
Think of laughter underground.
Roots twist and twirl with glee,
Celebrating their jubilee!

Embracing the Unseen

In the dark, the roots hold hands,
They weave jokes like elastic bands.
"Why do we grow down, not up?
Because diggin's more fun than a cup!"

The branches above can never know,
What secrets below prefer to show.
"You tickle me, let's laugh out loud,
While the world looks way too proud!"

Fungi dance with a sprightly cheer,
"No one sees, but we're all here!"
Together they conspire and plot,
Making mischief—who would've thought?

At twilight's fall, the magic's real,
A party that none can steal.
So here's to roots that laugh and play,
In their hidden world, come what may!

The Labyrinth of Leaves

In the garden, a maze we weave,
Chasing squirrels, they won't believe.
Branches twist like they have a plan,
But I trip over roots—oh, man!

A ladybug leads a tiny trail,
Whispering secrets, they never fail.
"Follow me," it seems to say,
But I'm lost—where's my way?

The daisies giggle in the breeze,
Mocking me, down on my knees.
Each turn I make, another laugh,
Oh, to find the right path, what a gaffe!

In this maze, I'm quite the jest,
Nature's puzzle, I try my best.
While I wander, the trees conspire,
To keep me lost, I must admire!

Nature's Hidden Knots

In the woods, a riddle grows,
With every twist, the laughter flows.
Vines tie themselves in quirky ways,
Playing tricks on sunny days.

A raccoon snickers from a tree,
"Hey buddy, come and play with me!"
But as I reach for a playful nut,
I trip and land, oh what a rut!

The bushes whisper jokes so sly,
Beneath the branches, giggles fly.
With every step, I dance and twirl,
Nature's knots make my head whirl.

Yet in this chaos, joy does sprout,
Finding laughter in every route.
Though I stumble and tumble around,
In hidden knots, my smiles are found!

Spirals of Serenity

Round and round, the petals sway,
In a spiral dance, they play.
Little bees buzz with delight,
In this whirl, I lose my sight.

Spinning flowers, what a sight,
Tickled by breezes, pure delight.
I twirl too, but slip and fall,
Laughter echoes, nature's call.

The sun beamed down to join the fun,
"Keep spinning, friend, you've just begun!"
I tried to follow the winding spree,
But they're all laughing—what's wrong with me?

Yet amidst the giggles and spins so free,
I find a rhythm, swaying with glee.
In this spiral, I take my chance,
Embracing nature's joyful dance!

Lush Embraces

In the thickets, hugs go wide,
Leaves wrap 'round like a leafy tide.
Each branch a friend, oh so sincere,
Nature's cuddles, always near.

I stumbled into a fussy shrub,
"Excuse me, did I disturb your club?"
The thorns just chuckled, not very mean,
And I laughed too—what a scene!

The ferns wave gently with a grin,
Welcoming all who wander in.
In this green embrace, what joy I find,
Nature's arms are truly kind.

So here I linger, warm and free,
Lost in laughter among the greenery.
With every hug from every tree,
Life's a giggle, just wait and see!

Boughs Binding the Spirit

In forests where the branches sway,
A squirrel dances, making hay.
With acorns launching through the air,
He thinks it's Christmas everywhere.

The vines are teasing at my toes,
As tangled up as garden hose.
I trip and tumble, what a sight!
But laughter greets my silly flight.

A bird has found a perfect hat,
Upon my head, the fluffy cat.
With twigs and leaves, I'm crowned a tree,
What's growing here? Oh, woe is me!

Yet every vine wraps me with glee,
In nature's trap, I shout, "Yippee!"
So here I'll dwell, amidst the green,
With pranks and jests, I rule this scene!

Variegated Paths

Through bushes thick, the hedgehog darts,
While shadows play with hidden arts.
Each step a gamble, what a game!
No path is right, they're all the same.

A froggy jumps, but misses seat,
And lands on flowers, oh, what a feat!
With all the colors blushing bright,
He croaks a tune, calls it goodnight.

The leaves conspire, they giggle loud,
While squirrels weave a leafy shroud.
Each twist and turn is pure delight,
In this mad maze of green and light.

When I emerge, a muddy mess,
I find I've won the jungle's guess.
Unruly paths, but oh, so true,
In nature's fun, forever blue!

The Embrace of Greenery

The ivy hugs the garden wall,
While daisies giggle, having a ball.
With every leaf, a wink, a cheer,
They shout, "Stay close, we're glad you're here!"

A dandelion dressed in gold,
Claims he's the best, or so I'm told.
He puffs and preens, a charming show,
While bees all buzz, "Oh, don't you know?"

In every nook, a secret's kept,
Where nature's jests have softly leapt.
Through tangled weeds with playful grace,
I find a smile upon my face.

So here I sit, amongst the cheer,
These leafy friends, I hold so dear.
In vibrant green, my heart takes flight,
With laughter echoing, pure delight!

Explorations in the Overgrowth

Amidst the wild, where tall grass creeps,
A brave explorer softly leaps.
With every step, a giggle borne,
As bushy tails and critters scorn.

The ladybug, all dressed in red,
Claims she's a queen upon my head.
With tiny wings, she winks at me,
Insects know the best, you see?

A bouncy beetle rolls a ball,
And all his friends begin to call.
In spiraled paths and leafy glades,
The games we play, the fun cascades.

Each twist and turn breeds joyful yells,
Where mischief lives, and laughter swells.
So let the wild forever roam,
In overgrowth, I find my home!

Secrets Beneath the Canopy

In a forest where secrets roam,
Squirrels gossip about their home.
Mice wear hats made of acorns,
While raccoons scheme for midnight returns.

The owls hoot riddles, wise and bright,
As fireflies dance in the moonlit night.
A hedgehog juggles, quite a show,
While turtles race, albeit slow.

Shadows of the Twisted Path

On the path where shadows play,
A rabbit hops in a silly way.
He wears a coat, polka-dotted too,
Singing songs about old kangaroo.

The trees lean in with a creaky grin,
Gossiping tales of the squirrel kin.
A dancing mushroom joins the fun,
Shouting loudly, 'I'm number one!'

Lattice of Longing

In a garden of whims, blooms do twirl,
A ladybug dreams of a fancy whirl.
A bee with a tie brings gossip sweet,
While daisies sway to a funky beat.

The vines are tangled, a playful mess,
Ballooning bumblebees start to confess.
They long for a dance under the sun,
With petals applauding the cozy fun.

The Weft of the Wild

In the wild where laughter sings,
A fox boasts of all his wings.
Though he can't fly, he leaps and bounds,
Chasing the chaos that always astounds.

The raccoons play poker under the stars,
While owls bet on the color of cars.
A funny little skunk rolls by in glee,
Announcing loudly, 'You can't catch me!'

The Ties That Bind

In a garden of shoes, quite the sight,
A cat in a hat, a dog in fright.
They leap over weeds, with giggles abound,
While socks and old gloves dance on the ground.

The gnomes join the fun, with their crooked spines,
They twist and they turn, in jolly designs.
With each little step, they trip on the grass,
Creating a ruckus, oh how they amass!

A swing in the air, a pie takes a flight,
Landing on grandma, what a strange sight!
Laughter erupts, as the birds sway along,
This messy bouquet, a comic relief song.

As chaos emerges, friendships grow tight,
In a jumble of laughter, all feels just right.
With every odd pairing, joy fills the space,
Life's tangled delight was never a race.

Serpentine Serenity

A snake on a swing, what a twisty affair,
With a grin like a child, floating up in the air.
It loops like a noodle, it dips down to play,
Making merry mischief, in its slithery way.

In the midst of the fun, a frog starts to croak,
Crafting odd tales, like a jester's old joke.
Bouncing from leaf to leaf, oh so spry,
While whispering secrets that slip from the sky.

The sun slips away, wearing shades of bright hue,
As the creatures get cozy, in laughter askew.
A party in shadows, where giggles abound,
Among whims and wonders, joy knows no bound.

With wiggles and wobbles, they dance on a line,
Each creature claiming a slice of the shine.
In this playful circus, where chaos is king,
Serenity thrives in the laughter they bring.

Entwined in Silence

A hedgehog in boots, it tiptoes in glee,
Wishing to join in, a grand jamboree.
With prickle and laughter, it softly shushes,
While a snail in a shell, lightly blushes.

A quiet parade, with a giggling breeze,
Sees critters convene beneath tangled trees.
Whispers of joy in a snug little crowd,
As silence tickles, feeling less proud.

A squirrel up high, turns around with a frown,
A missed acorn drop, leads to fits of brown.
With laughter erupting, it twirls in its place,
Creating a ruckus while losing the race.

In shadows they gather, their stories collide,
Each secret shared, like a thrilling ride.
In hushed little chuckles, their peace intertwines,
Finding bliss in the quiet, beneath hidden vines.

Flourishing Chaos

In a field full of flowers, a bee takes a spin,
Spilling its nectar with swirls of a grin.
Petals collide, in a burst of delight,
As butterflies giggle, taking flight.

The wind plays a tune, as the daisies sway,
While a squirrel with flair flips in dismay.
He aims for a branch, but oh, what a fall,
Landing in laughter, he invites them all.

A dance through the meadows, where mischief is found,
The playful antics of nature astound.
Each blossom a giggle, each fragrance a tease,
In this chaotic bloom, everyone sees.

With colors a'blazing, and joy on the loose,
Life's circus unfolds, with each silly excuse.
In flourishing chaos, a riot of cheer,
Every petal and laugh brings us all near.

Twists of Time

In the garden, socks gone awry,
Dancing with weeds, oh me, oh my!
The clock spins round, a dizzy dance,
Lost in a wash, a sock's romance.

A spatula flies, a cake takes flight,
Baking disasters, oh what a sight!
The past rolls back, in flour and fun,
Who knew time travel's this easily done?

The cat in a hat, perched on a chair,
Whiskers twitching, does he even care?
A leap through the air, with a tumble and roll,
Where do they go, when they lose control?

In twisted gardens, we find our place,
Laughter erupts, a joyful race!
With each silly turn, life spins around,
In gloves of mismatched shades, joy's found.

Braided Journeys

Three friends embark on a quest so grand,
With noodle maps held in each hand.
They wander paths of licorice trees,
Searching for snacks on a hot summer's breeze.

Each step they take, a slip and a slide,
Rolling down hills with giggles worldwide.
Their shadows twist into silly shapes,
Lions and giraffes made of grapes!

A squirrel joins with an acorn hat,
Offering wisdom on where to find that.
He spins tales of mischief and fun,
As the sun sets, their laughter's begun.

Winding through tales that spark delight,
What a journey, what a sight!
With braided paths like spaghetti strands,
Exploring the world, hand in hand.

Threads of Enchantment

Frogs in tophats sing their tune,
Under the glow of a cheese moon.
They croak in chorus, a symphony strange,
As the world around them starts to change.

A needle passes through a quirky quilt,
Stitching stories with colorful silt.
Each thread appears as a whimsical tale,
Spinning giggles, never to fail.

Marshmallows float in a fizzy stream,
A candy land born from a daydream.
With laughter woven into each seam,
In this realm, all is not what it seems.

Through patterns of joy, and colors so bright,
The fabric of life dances in light.
With every stitch, magic ignites,
Threads of wonder in whimsical flights.

The Snare of Connection

Caught in a web of spaghetti strings,
They dined on humor, laughter it brings.
With meatballs rolling all over the floor,
What a mess, but who could ask for more?

Best friends share tales, a playful tease,
Drawing laughter like honey from bees.
They craft connections with jellybean glue,
Binding their hearts like a gumdrop crew.

A mishap here, a pratfall there,
Their bond grows strong with every flare.
Through pies in the face and games gone wild,
Each silly moment, they're joyfully filed.

Through sticky moments of sweet delight,
Together they shine, forever so bright.
In the snare of connection, they find their way,
As laughter echoes, come what may.

Overgrown Secrets

In the garden, weeds have plans,
They gossip without any hands.
Chasing bugs and birds, oh my,
As daisies giggle, passing by.

In corners, mysteries sprout,
With tangled thoughts, they scream and shout.
Laughter hides beneath the soil,
As chaos dances in the toil.

The car roots do the shimmy,
While ants hold a lively mini.
With petals twirling, brave and free,
Nature's circus, come and see!

A sunflower's hat, askew and bold,
Participates in secrets told.
Beneath the leaves, whispers tread,
Of wild ideas sprouting from bed.

A Dance of the Green

Fern fronds wave like arms in glee,
While beetles host a jubilee.
A waltz of weeds, a shimmy bright,
Underneath the pale moonlight.

Silly mushrooms jump and twirl,
As crickets serenade and whirl.
Lettuce pirouettes in the breeze,
Tickled by the buzzing bees.

Grassy blades do the cha-cha,
While dandelions say, 'Ha-HA!'
With roots entwined in merry jest,
Every plant believes it's blessed.

In this riot of hues and strains,
Even earthworms join the trains.
A lovely show, so bright and keen,
Where every leaf's a dancing queen!

Roots in the Mist

Beneath the fog, the roots conspire,
To plot a tale that won't expire.
With laughter bubbling deep below,
They twist in knots, putting on a show.

Whispering plots in murky ways,
Each trying to steal the other's praise.
A tic-tac-toe of tangled pines,
Entwining vines share punchline signs.

Hiccups from the muddy ground,
Crack a joke and all around.
A beetle slips—a comic slip,
As roots all cheer, and take a dip.

So here they grow—a secret crew,
The laughter spreading in the dew.
In foggy plots so sly and keen,
Roots dance unseen in shades of green.

Convolutions of Time

Yesterday's seedlings, bold and spry,
   Flip through pages of the sky.
  Giggling branches, quite the sight,
    Mimic shadows in the light.

Twirling memories in the breeze,
  Whispering tales of bumblebees.
   Time giggles in the garden bed,
As old roots tease the sprout instead.

Winding clocks from insects' wings,
   Create the rhythm—joy it brings.
    A melody of green and brown,
    As laughter tumbles all around.

With every twist, each loop, and curl,
   Life swirls like a dervish whirl.
  The garden hums a timeless rhyme,
    In every crevice, echoes chime.

Embrace of the Unraveled

In a twisty embrace of vines so spry,
A squirrel found itself in a high-flying tie.
With acorns galore, it had lots to munch,
But how to escape? It just couldn't hunch.

The neighbors all laughed as it darted about,
Doing cartwheels and flips without a doubt.
Its tail flapped wildly, a comical sight,
A circus of chaos in the morning light.

Finally, with grace, it broke free from the fray,
And scuttled away like a star in the play.
Boughs swayed with laughter, the woodpeckers cheered,
That sneaky little critter had the crowd truly steered.

Thus nature's show painted the park with delight,
As vines spun the tales of a curious flight.
Each creature would chuckle, eyes wide with glee,
In this glorious mess, the world felt so free.

Clutch of the Creep

In shadows so thick where the branches entwine,
 A snake with ambitions, oh, isn't it fine?
It slithered and bloomed in an awkward parade,
 With a wiggle and giggle, it thought it was made.

But oh, what a tangle, the leaves couldn't hide,
 As it tripped on its tail, feeling less than dignified.
With a bounce and a twist, it went off on a spree,
 Dodging laughter and light, oh, how free it could be!

The rabbits stood tall, clutching bellies with pain,
 Their chuckles erupted like a sunshiney rain.
"Careful, dear friend!" cried the wise, furry sage,
 "For a clumsy critter brings giggles, not rage!"

So the snake took a bow, slapping ferns with flair,
And vowed next time round it would surely take care.
With a wiggle, a chuckle, it slid back to its hole,
 In the clutch of the creep, it had regained its role.

Interlocking Stories

In a meadow where daisies and stories collide,
A rabbit and turtle had tales to provide.
With hops and slow walks, they swapped all their lore,
In laughter and sighs, they found so much more.

"Your speed is a gift," said the turtle with pride,
"But slow and steady wins the race," he replied.
The rabbit just chuckled, "I hop with such glee,
But I love your wisdom, oh can you see?"

They interlocked tales of both victory and woe,
With sunbeams a-dancing, their joy began to grow.
From the sprint of a bush to the pause of a creek,
Their stories unfolded, each brilliant and unique.

So under the sky, with a nod and a wink,
They laughed over clovers, not daring to blink.
Two friends in a meadow where the stories lay wide,
Finding fun in the place where their worlds would collide.

The Burden of the Boughs

Boughs heavy with fruit, quite a marvelous sight,
Yet a parrot in search found its wings felt so tight.
It flew into branches, an aerial dance,
But soon it was stuck, oh, what a mischance!

With a squawk and a flap, it tried to unwind,
Wrapping itself in leaves, a real twisty bind.
The critters all gathered—what a comical show,
As the parrot proclaimed, "I'm stuck, don't you know?"

The squirrel tossed peanuts, a snack to appease,
While the rabbit just snorted, aiming hard for a tease.
"Don't worry, my friend! Just shake it off quick!
It's just a bad tangle, not some magic trick!"

Then with one final flap and a powerful shout,
The parrot unfurled, sending leaves all about.
With a flourish it soared, leaving all in a daze,
In the boughs' wild embrace, it danced a new phase.

Links of the Eternal Green

In the garden, vines do twist,
Chasing sunlight, they can't resist.
They dance and sway, a comical crew,
Waving hello to the morning dew.

A dandelion's ambitions loom,
While weeds conspire in the room.
Caterpillars take a fashion spree,
Wearing leaves as hats, fancy and free.

Bouncing beetles roll around,
While ants march on, they're quite profound.
The squirrels giggle, oh what a sight,
As acorns tumble, an airborne fright.

In nature's maze, it's all a game,
Where every creature shares a name.
With laughter echoing through the green,
The finest show you've ever seen.

Breeze Through the Gnarls

Rusty branches wave and tease,
A quirky concert on the breeze.
Gnarled roots play peek-a-boo,
While birds chirp tales, loud and true.

The foxes prance in joyful race,
With wildflowers caught in their embrace.
Caterwauling, the owls hoot,
Squeaky boots, this is their loot.

A breeze blows through, we all sway,
Tickling leaves in a merry display.
The wind hums tunes, a silly song,
Inviting all to sing along.

Under the canopy, what a show!
Every leaf seems to steal the glow.
Nature's circus, full of cheer,
A wobbly spectacle, oh dear, oh dear!

Liquid Latticework

Streamers of green in the creek do flow,
A jolly river with a bubbly glow.
Fish in bow ties swim with flair,
While frogs juggle flies, if they dare.

Bubbles rise like balloons in glee,
As turtles dive, 'Hey, look at me!'
Marshmallows cloud in the bright blue,
A picnic party, just for the few.

Wiggle and giggle, the ripples spread,
As ducks tell jokes, here's what they said:
"Why did the lily pad sit in the shade?
Too hot for comfort, it got dismayed!"

Nature's laughter echoes wide,
In the liquid dance where joy cannot hide.
Water's embrace, with giggles entwined,
A silky tapestry, whimsically designed.

The Clutches of Nature

In the garden's tight embrace,
A squirrel scurries, what a race!
With acorns in hand, it plots away,
For a nutty feast on a sunny day.

Raccoons masquerade as bandit kings,
Raiding kitchens for leftover things.
With little paws and masked delight,
They scurry off into the night.

Plants gossip as they grow tall,
Whispering secrets to each sprawl.
The sunbeams tickle, they sway and bend,
In nature's play, the fun won't end.

Oh, the clutches of greenery fair,
Catch you laughing without a care.
In this riotous realm, full of flair,
Every leaf has a joke to share.

Resilience in the Tangle

In the mirror of the trees, I find,
A branch winks, it's feeling kind.
A squirrel's dart, a duck's dismay,
Leaves play tag, joy on display.

Knotty vines with stories told,
Laughing bugs, so brave and bold.
A crow's caw breaks the merry cheer,
While shadows dance, we've no real fear.

Twists and turns, a maze of green,
I trip on roots, yet feel serene.
The sun peeks through the leafy maze,
Nature giggles, in whimsical ways.

In chaos, we discover grace,
Through each stumble, a smiling face.
Life's a jigsaw, oddly spread,
Yet every piece fits, it's joy instead.

The Curve of Companionship

Two worms wiggle, side by side,
Through muddy paths, they take their stride.
Their laughter fills the damp, cool air,
A friendship formed, with squirming flair.

A clumsy ant shows off her dance,
Unclear of steps, but full of chance.
While ladybugs in spots of red,
Cheer for her as they bob their head.

Together, they stumble, fumble, and fall,
In chaotic joy, they have a ball.
The world looks different close to the ground,
With giggles and wiggles, love profound.

Under glowing stars, they share their dreams,
A chorus of whispers, laughter beams.
Through every curve, each twist and bend,
Life's a riddle, with friends to lend.

The Interplay of Shadows

A shadow lurks with mischief bright,
Sliding quickly, just out of sight.
It steals my snack, how rude of it!
My sunny day turned into a skit.

Swaying grasses whisper and tease,
Their playful giggles dance on the breeze.
While colors mingle in a dizzy swirl,
A shy sunbeam grins, starts to twirl.

In the hiding spots, giggles arise,
Bouncing light plays in disguise.
As shadows poke their silly heads,
The ground is painted with laughter spreads.

A game of hide-and-seek ensues,
Who will trick, and who'll get to choose?
In the playful knots of shadow play,
I realize, it's all a grand ballet.

Momentum of the Underbrush

Beneath the brush, a riot grows,
With clumsy leaps, a raccoon shows.
Chasing tails, they skip and slide,
In a messy burst, they confide.

The bigger beasts, they laugh aloud,
As tiny critters form a crowd.
With each rustle, they join the race,
A comical, boisterous, bushy chase.

A plucky fox flips, stumbles wide,
While badgers cheer from their cozy hide.
A splash of mud, a bark, a cheer,
Every misstep brings the fun near.

In a wilderness that's wild and free,
Each bump and tumble, a jubilee.
The underbrush thrills in its own style,
As laughter echoes for mile after mile.

The Braided Path

Two squirrels dance on branches high,
One trips and starts to fly.
A laugh erupts, the forest shakes,
As acorns drop, oh, what a break!

The path is twisted, like my hair,
With every turn, I feel the dare.
Donkeys walk a straightened line,
While I take twists, it's all divine!

A rabbit winks, as if to say,
"Through loops we go, hip-hip-hooray!"
But watch your step, it's quite a feat,
With all these leaves beneath my feet.

A spider spins, his web so grand,
He tries to catch a peanut band.
Bouncing bugs just wave goodnight,
And scatter off in sheer delight!

Wild Connections

A hedgehog rolls, a true delight,
He thinks he's stealthy in the night.
But owls chuckle from above,
"What a mess, my little love!"

The bees are buzzing, making plans,
To throw a party with their bands.
But sticky paws get in the way,
A jammed-up hive, a funny play!

The frogs discuss their latest cast,
While fluttering by, the snail moves fast.
"Here comes trouble, slow but bold!"
A wild affair, a tale retold.

A raccoon dons a dish for flair,
Pretending he's the grandest heir.
But inside jokes and playful pranks,
Make our forest full of thanks!

Forest Cradle

A treehouse swings, the forest sighs,
As monkeys race beneath the skies.
One slips and lands on mossy green,
And giggles burst, a comical scene.

The owls debate who's up at night,
While fireflies offer glowing light.
With tiny hats and tiny shoes,
They hold a ball, they cannot lose!

Raccoons sneak in with stealthy moves,
Looking for snacks, they've got the grooves.
But in the end, they face defeat,
As the snacks vanish and they retreat.

A breeze whispers secrets low,
While nature's children put on a show.
In this cradle where laughter blooms,
We find our joy amidst the glooms!

Bonds Beneath the Canopy

A caterpillar's quite the sight,
He scoffs, "I'll fly, just wait till night!"
His friends all laugh, it's quite the tale,
As he just munches on the trail.

The wind heaves whispers, rustles leaves,
While chatter weaves through tangled eaves.
A family of birds makes quite a fuss,
As squirrels tease and make a muss.

The fox swears he's a chef, you see,
With nuts and berries, fish for free.
But when he tastes, he makes a face,
"The only dish? A dreadful chase!"

In this woodland, bonds we find,
With laughter shared and hearts entwined.
From races run to chats at dusk,
In every moment, life's a bust!

Twisted Ancestry

In a garden where gnomes dance,
A vine took a curious stance.
It wrapped around pots with flair,
Creating a green, leafy hair.

Uncles are squirrels, so it seems,
Aunties are flowers, with odd dreams.
Family gatherings get quite weird,
When petals and nuts are what they cheered.

Every branch tells a tale of its kin,
Peeking out where the sun's getting in.
Grandma's a cactus, pricking my side,
A jest in the jungle, a playful ride.

But deeper we delve, and what do we find?
A cousinly marshmallow, quite well-defined!
All tangled up, yet a mix so sweet,
Our roots all entwined, what a comical feat!

The Clasp of the Foliage

In the woods where the wild things play,
Leaves hug branches in a quirky way.
A bud laughed loud, said, "Hey, look at me!"
While stems did the cha-cha, quite carefree!

They clasp and they twirl, make merry of flaws,
Chatting with critters, and even the paws.
Oh, nature's embrace, a humorous sight,
With foliage gossiping morning to night.

Laughter erupts from an acorn so spry,
"Why grow up too fast? Just give it a try!"
The branches all giggle, in sun and in rain,
While roots tell their jokes, with no sense of shame.

Leaves play a game of hide-and-seek,
While the wind whispers secrets, all giggles and squeaks.
A vine does a flip, with a comical grace,
In the clasp of the foliage, we all find our place.

Fragments of the Interlace

In a web of odd shapes, so jumbled and neat,
Socks get entangled beneath my own feet.
The cat leaps and tumbles, all up in the fray,
Chasing after shadows that hide in the play.

A spider with jokes spins threads of delight,
Tickling the fringes, making me giggle at night.
Mismatched patterns, they sparkle and shine,
These fragments of chaos, truly divine!

Caught in the net are my lost little things,
Like mittens and marbles, oh what joy it brings!
They mingle and merge, in a twisty ballet,
A yarn of the laughter that brightens the day.

So here's to the mess, to the ruckus we weave,
Finding fun in the chaos, oh, you better believe!
With every odd tangle, a giggle takes flight,
Fragments of moments that dance in delight.

Paths of the Once Lost

In a forest of giggles and quirks galore,
Paths overlap, become something more.
A lost shoe sings a tune of the past,
While sticks tell their tales, oh my, what a blast!

The map of mischief unfurls in the breeze,
Leading us, wandering, with whimsical ease.
A roller coaster ride on a path made of leaves,
With laughter and joy sewn into the thieves.

Once lost, now found, they trot back with flair,
Mischief on horseback, through sun and through air.
Each twist in the trail brings a chuckle to share,
As antics come tumbling, unweighted by care.

So follow the laughter, the pathways so bold,
With stories a-plenty, like treasures of old.
In the paths of the once lost, we find our way,
A tapestry woven with giggles that play!

Whispers of the Entwined

In the garden, vines conspire,
Jokes and jests, they never tire.
One tickles leaves, the other shouts,
Laughter's music, round about.

With every twist, a secret shared,
A plan concocted, none prepared.
A fruit here snores, a flower giggles,
Their silly dance, oh how it wiggles!

Beneath the sun, they stretch and play,
An afternoon, where greenery sways.
Buds exchange lines, comedic flair,
Nature's stand-up, without a care.

As shadows grow, they take a bow,
For tonight's show, they'll wow the crowd.
In roots and shoots, the humor spreads,
A vine of laughter, where joy treads.

The Emblem of Togetherness

Two branches dance in the soft breeze,
Chasing squirrels, with skill and ease.
One slips up, a comic fall,
The other hoots, a laughing call.

A knot of leaves, in playful fight,
Wrapped in giggles, pure delight.
They play charades, but none can see,
What tales are spun in harmony.

Sunshine beams on a wide embrace,
They stumble over roots in place.
Yet every trip just brings more cheer,
Together, they conquer all their fear.

As dusk unfolds, their shadows blend,
In every twist, they find a friend.
For life's a jest when shared with glee,
A jolly bond, as tough as tea.

The Grasp of Old Roots

Roots below weave quite a tale,
Of clumsy critters and winds that wail.
A beetle slips, it starts to roll,
While ants unite to take control.

In earthy hugs, they laugh aloud,
Old roots, a wise and silly crowd.
They reminisce of rainy days,
And pranks they've pulled in curious ways.

A cozy nook for bugs to chat,
Gossip flies where soil is at.
They share a sprite, a giggle or two,
Old stories shine like morning dew.

When storms come in with rumbling might,
Their grip on fun will hold them tight.
In muddy puddles, joy reveals,
The grasp of friends, where laughter heals.

Entwined Fates

Two paths cross under leafy skies,
Branches clash with playful sighs.
One says, "Let's reach the sun today!"
The other laughs, "But I can't play!"

Their stubborn bends create a scene,
A comic stretch like none have seen.
They race with wind, both full of cheer,
But always trip when moon draws near.

Vines argue on whose way is best,
A friendly tug-of-war, no rest.
The sun looks on, stifling grins,
As roots entwine, and mischief begins.

When stars appear, they intertwine,
In cosmic dance, perfectly fine.
For life, dear friend, is best in jest,
Where fanciful paths lead to the rest.

The Growth of Kinship

In the garden of laughter, we sprout,
With roots intertwined, there's no doubt.
We trip on the hose, and start to roll,
Family is chaos, but that's how we stroll.

Each cousin's a seed, sown wild and free,
With petals of jokes, they bloom with glee.
We water our quirks with stories old,
In this patch of humor, we're rich with gold.

Bumblebees buzz with a comical hum,
As we dance in sunlight, we wiggle and strum.
The weeds are our friends, they laugh in the shade,
In this flowering mess, our bonds are made.

So here's to the roots, and the laughs they bring,
In the soil of our hearts, let the joy ever swing.
Through the muck and the mire, we find our way,
Growing together, come what may.

The Mists of the Thicket

In the thicket of whimsy, we frolic around,
A maze of madcap in the underbrush found.
Twigs like silly hats, we wear with flair,
Lost in the laughter, without a care.

The shadows whisper jokes, wrapped in green,
Squirrels are giggling; it's quite the scene.
We chase after giggles, like leaves in the breeze,
Clothing ourselves in the laughter of trees.

A mist of mirth blankets the ground,
With each step forward, new giggles abound.
The branches above join in with their laugh,
Spreading joy like a sweet photograph.

In every corner, a chuckle takes flight,
In this thicket of laughter, the world feels just right.
With friends by our side, through the fog we glide,
In this whimsical thicket, we take stride.

The Braid of Time

In the loom of life, threads twist and twine,
Fun moments blend into the grand design.
A rowdy stitch sends a giggle along,
Woven with memories, where all belong.

Zany patterns emerge in the dance,
Where fate and folly take a peculiar chance.
Each loop is a chuckle, each knot is a grin,
In the fabric of friendship, joy lies within.

As the clock tick-tocks, mischief we make,
Through the seams of our laughter, the world we awake.
Time's a great prankster, with jokes of its own,
In the braid of our journey, we're never alone.

So gather the threads, come weave with us here,
A tapestry vibrant with glee and cheer.
With each twist and turn, let's celebrate rhyme,
In the colorful weave of the braid called time.

Whorls of Longing

In the garden of dreams, spirals unfurl,
Each wish is a petal, each thought a twirl.
Bumbles and giggles float high on the air,
In a dance of delight, we swirl without care.

Like vines we entwine, in a playful jest,
Shooting for laughter, we're truly blessed.
The sun winks down at our silly parade,
In this carousel of wishes, let's never fade.

Twirling in circles, we chase after fun,
With the wind as our partner, we'll never outrun.
A pinch of nostalgia, a sprinkle of cheer,
In the whorls of our hearts, we'll hold it all dear.

So let's dance in the sun, with our dreams in the sky,
In this playful spiral, we're destined to fly.
With laughter our compass, and silliness true,
In the whorls of longing, I'm glad to have you.

The Weaving of Fate

In a garden of whims, fate does play,
Threads of laughter twist and sway.
Colors collide in chaos galore,
Who knew a patchwork could mean so much more?

With each stitch, a giggle ensues,
A cat with a hat dances in shoes.
Fabric of folly, cut from the same cloth,
Sewing up smiles, we all have a scoff.

Patterns emerge that don't quite fit,
The tailor is lost in a fabric of wit.
Stitches of humor that can't quite refrain,
In this playful quilt, we all entertain.

Fate's mischief is woven so bright,
As mismatched socks bring pure delight.
Who'd have thought yarn could be such a game?
In the weaving of fate, we're all quite the same.

Frayed Edges of Memory

Memories dangle, a frayed little thread,
A laugh at the moment, now lost or misread.
Who ate the last bite of grandma's pie?
Oh wait! It was me - why oh why?

In the attic of thought, dust bunnies play,
Twisting old tales that refuse to decay.
A sock on the ceiling, quite out of place,
Memories giggle, full of grace.

Hats made of hair, oh what a sight!
Eccentric ideas that took off in flight.
The edges may fray, but the laughter won't cease,
In the fabric of recollection, we find our peace.

So here's to the moments, both silly and sweet,
Where the past and the present are always a treat.
Even when tangled, let's cherish the mess,
For frayed edges of memory, we love to confess.

Vines of Intrigue

Winding and twisting, a plot so absurd,
Whispers of secrets, yet no one has heard.
A grapevine with gossip, just ripe for the bite,
Entwined in the story, stuck in plain sight.

Bumbling along in this maze of delight,
A sly little rabbit darts in and out of the night.
Each turn reveals laughter, a riddle or two,
In vines of intrigue, we giggle anew.

The gardener chuckles, says, "Not my fault!"
As he trips on the roots, does a comical vault.
Nature's own tricks bring us silly surprise,
With vines of intrigue, no truth melts in guise.

So dance with the shadows, get lost in the cheer,
For in these wild tangles, we find what we fear.
Let's pluck at the strings, let the laughter be free,
In the vines of intrigue, we're all meant to be.

Knots in the Fabric

Oh look, what a jumble, it's twisted like thought,
Knots in the fabric, a treasure we sought.
A button that vanished, where could it be?
Lost in the stitches, laughing with glee.

The seamstress is giggling, can't find her way,
As patterns get muddled in the fabric of play.
A patch here and there, it's a fun little map,
Each kink tells a story, a whimsical clap.

We tug at the threads, and they pull back in jest,
Each knot that we find is our very best quest.
With fabric so silly, what joy now unfolds,
In knots that we dress, absurdity beholds.

So let's tie up our dreams in a snug little bow,
With knots in the fabric, let the laughter flow.
In this colorful chaos, together we stand,
For life's little messes are truly quite grand.

Echoes of Entwined Journeys

In the garden of whimsy, under bright skies,
A snail races past with a look of surprise.
Two vines hold hands, plotting their spree,
While a gopher digs deep for a cup of sweet tea.

The daisies keep giggling, gossiping low,
As a butterfly stumbles, stealing the show.
The wind plays a tune only branches can hear,
And laughter takes flight, spreading much cheer.

Chasing the shadows, a frog jumps in glee,
Hopping on thistles, so wild and so free.
With each bounce and twist, a tale unfolds,
In the land of green, where nonsense is gold.

Petunias wear hats, parade down the lane,
While a ladybug grins, knowing no pain.
Amidst the bright colors, life dances and spins,
In this tangled-up world, everyone wins.

The Twist of Fate

A critter named Larry was craving a snack,
But found himself stuck in a vine's silly track.
He wiggled and squirmed, oh what a sight,
As the garden erupted in laughter that night.

A pair of old turtles looked on with delight,
One said, 'Dear Larry, you'll be here till twilight!'
But Larry just chuckled, 'It's all in good fun,
Just wait for my twist, I'll be fast like the sun.'

With a flip and a flop, he made quite a jump,
Leaving behind all of the dread and the slump.
But as fate would have it, the next vine was near,
And back to the start, he'd appear with a cheer.

So round and around, the cycle would go,
With nature's sweet jesters, put on quite the show.
And Larry, well, bless him, he'd dance all the way,
In this wacky, wild twist where all frogs laugh and play.

Veils of Verdant Life

In a patch of green where the sunlight weaves,
A mouse named Morty plays tricks with the leaves.
He hides in the ferns, with a giggle so bright,
While a squirrel nearby tests his acorn's flight.

The flowers all chat, with petals aglow,
'Have you seen Morty? Just look at him go!'
He pops out of nowhere, a prank in his paws,
And everyone chuckles at his silly flaws.

Then comes a rabbit, with ears all askew,
Who trips on a root, creating a view.
The whole garden laughs, such a jolly parade,
While nature's own circus provides the charade.

Beneath all the leaves, life's chaos reveals:
Jokes made of shadows, long laughter appeals.
In this green, tangled web, nothing's quite straight,
As the joy of the earth swirls around with fate.

Woven Stories of the Earth

Once in a meadow, where stories are spun,
An ant called Alonzo declared, 'I've just won!'
He found a lost crumb and danced all around,
While others looked on, completely spellbound.

The grasshoppers chirped a disheveled tune,
As the sunlit beams danced under the moon.
But Alonzo, distracted, forgot where to flee,
And bonded with daisies in sheer jubilee.

With twirls and with swirls, he led quite the show,
Inviting more creatures, 'Come join, don't be slow!'
So around them they laughed, a magnificent blend,
Sharing their tales as daylight would end.

In circles they spun, in a whirl of delight,
Leaving behind worries, embracing the night.
Life's woven stories, with laughter and cheer,
In a patchwork of wonders that brings us all near.

Whimsy in the Wiry Stalks

In a garden where odd things grow,
Curly beets put on a show.
With sprouting radishes dressed so bright,
They dance around, what a silly sight!

The carrots prance with floppy hats,
Mischievous squirrels tie them in spats.
Beneath the sun, they giggle and tease,
Nudging each other like old friends at ease.

Tomatoes roll down a leafy slide,
While cucumbers peek, they can't hide.
Pumpkins joke with a squash so spry,
Launching seeds in a flying high.

In this patch, laughter takes its flight,
Bouncing shadows in the warm sunlight.
With every twist and playful grumble,
Nature's comedy makes hearts stumble!

The Confluence of Growth

In the bent of the lush green space,
Mighty beans have a winding race.
They climb and shimmy, what a show,
Competing with peas, who'll steal the glow?

Kale laughs out loud, "I've got the style!"
Radishes roll and say, "Stay awhile!"
"Mustard greens offer a tangy twist,
Join our frolic, you don't want to miss!"

Zucchini wiggles in a funky dance,
While garlic cloves chant, 'Take a chance!'
Together they form a quirky crew,
In the lively blend, there's so much to do.

As the veggies tumble, spiral, and shout,
In unity's laughter, there's never a doubt.
For in this garden of whimsy divine,
Each sprout and leaf knows how to shine!

Entwined Dreams

In a patch where dreams have grown,
Spaghetti squash declares, "I'm known!"
While beets and carrots share their tales,
Wrapped in greens like snuggly veils.

With a flutter and twist, the onions sing,
A chorus of layers and sweet spring bling.
They giggle soft, "Don't cry, dear friend,
We're all mixed up, but we'll mend!"

Potatoes roll with a charming flair,
Peppers shout, "We're a colorful pair!"
In this quirky blend, who needs a scheme?
For in every sprout lies a whimsical dream.

The vines embrace in a messy cheer,
No room for worries, only good beer!
In this garden of laughter, oh so bright,
Each silly sprout bounces in delight!

Undulating Currents

Beneath the surface where secrets hide,
Cucumbers and peppers take a wild ride.
They twirl and twist in the sun's warm spree,
Creating waves in this lively sea.

Radishes whisper, "Shh, don't spill a word,"
While squashes giggle, a little absurd.
Each leafy friend caught in the flow,
A merry band of veggies in a glow.

As they ripple and sway, mischief stirs,
Nudging each other with giggling purrs.
Tomatoes blush at the wave's soft kiss,
In this horticultural dance, there's no miss!

In the ebb and flow, all worries cease,
As the garden hums with playful peace.
Every twist and turn, a laughter-filled song,
In these undulating currents, we all belong!

Interwoven Whispers

In a bramble where squirrels race,
A hedgehog sneezes, oh what a face!
With vines that twist like silly mimes,
They giggle and dance through leafy climes.

A rabbit wearing glasses quite round,
Lost in a map he hasn't found.
The mossy floor, a trampoline,
Bouncing and laughing, quite the scene!

A frog sings loudly, not a good tune,
Chasing a fly that's too close to moon.
The bees all buzz in a silly way,
Holding a dance-off, hip-hip-hooray!

Each leaf that rustles has jokes to tell,
Of wiggly worms in their squishy shell.
With whispers and chuckles in joyous spree,
Nature's own comedy, wild and free!

The Hunter's Thicket

In the thicket, a nimble hare,
Wears a cap that's quite debonair.
He tiptoes past a snoozing bear,
With dreams of pastries in the air.

A hunter stalks with much finesse,
But finds himself in quite the mess.
His camouflage leaves him quite exposed,
As butterflies make him their grand host.

With boots all muddy and shirt askew,
He trips on roots that bid adieu.
A field mouse chuckles from a tall blade,
Holding the secret, it won't invade!

An owl hoots loudly, "What's the thrill?"
As the hunter rolls down the hill.
In nature's arms, with laughter free,
The greatest hunt is hilarity!

The Clutch of the Forest Floor

In the clutch of moss, a secret nest,
Where ants have gathered for a quest.
With tiny helmets and tiny wheels,
They hold a race, not the best of deals.

A snail with swagger, slow and grand,
Claims to be the fastest in the land.
While acorns nod, they think it's fun,
As mushrooms giggle and bask in sun.

A little fox trying to blend,
In hues of brown that twist and bend.
He stumbles as he tries to evade,
A chipmunk's game, oh what a charade!

At twilight's glow, the laughter swells,
As critters share their quirky spells.
The forest floor, a stage so bright,
Where every creature finds delight!

Secrets in the Grove

In the grove where shadows play,
A raccoon plots to steal the day.
With sticky fingers and a grin so wide,
He sneaks through grass and tries to hide.

A wise old owl squawks with glee,
"Who stole my snacks? Oh, let me see!"
While squirrels giggle, springing around,
Leaving little footprints, all over the ground.

The frogs are croaking a silly tune,
Under the light of a glowing moon.
With secrets whispered on the breeze,
They craft a romp that brings to knees!

Each branch holds tales of mirth and cheer,
From nuts to fruits, they hold so dear.
In every nook, a story thrives,
In the grove, everyone's alive!

A Symphony of Strands

In a garden where socks like to mate,
A left one and right can't find their fate.
They wiggle and squirm, oh what a sight,
In a dance of confusion, they take flight.

They gossip like birds on the clothesline wire,
"Whose turn is it to be in the dryer?"
A symphony played on a squeaky old rack,
While their partners are lost—oh, where are they at?

The Weaving of Worlds

A chair full of yarn, oh what a mess,
Knitting their dreams, but it's anyone's guess.
They twist and they turn, a colorful spree,
Creating a sweater for a cat named Louie.

The pattern's a puzzle, what could it be?
An ocean of chaos or a grand marquee?
Each stitch is a tale of mischief and fun,
In a world made of wool, the laughter's never done.

Whispers of Knotted Roots

In the forest, the vines laugh and twine,
Sharing their tales over lemony wine.
"Did you hear the news?" one cheeky vine grins,
"We're hosting a party with mushrooms and sins!"

The trees shake their branches, "Good luck with the dance!
Last time you tangled, you ruined our chance!"
Yet still they giggle, a riotous cheer,
As they get ready for fun and some beer.

Entangled Echoes

In a room where the cords like to play,
The speaker's been muted, what a cliché!
They tangle and twist, forming new shapes,
"Let's start a band," says the one with the grapes.

The echoes of laughter bounce off the walls,
As they form a conga, ignoring the calls.
They dance through the chaos with zany delight,
In a melody wild, where disorder feels right.

www.ingramcontent.com/pod-product-compliance
Lightning Source LLC
Chambersburg PA
CBHW050307120526
44590CB00016B/2523